Abstract

William Blake's works incorporate Eastern elements to challenge Western art, as seen in "The Spiritual Form of Pitt Guiding Behemoth" and "The Spiritual Form of Nelson Guiding Leviathan." These pieces raise questions about the true personality of these 'heroes' and the potential cultural appropriation resulting from the British Empire's presence in India.

Contents

Introduction 7

I. From Exhibitions to Artworks 11

II. Myths and Mythologies: Links in Similarity 27

III. Los and Brahma: Reshaping the Boundaries
      of Western Art 33

Conclusion 39

Bibliography 45

Introduction

A person like William Blake is destined to be extraordinary. His uniqueness does not stem from the value of his multiple identities as a poet, artist, and more, but rather from his ideas, his mind, and his thoughts.

He refers to his artworks as "eternal fantasies." For him, painting is a visual form of expressing his understanding of ultimate truth. The same goes for his poetry. His works cannot be scrutinised and interpreted from a single perspective; they are inevitably a comprehensive course involving religion, morality, philosophy, and politics.[1] Blake's expression of thoughts is complex and obscure, like a Nine Rings Puzzle from the East that must be unraveled ring by ring to glimpse its mysteries.

To understand Blake's ideas, Eastern civilisation serves as a necessary entry point. It is almost certain that Blake's works have an inseparable relationship with the East—or rather, his understanding of the East. David Weir explicitly states in his work "Bhrama in the West" how India subconsciously influenced Blake's creations. Particularly in Blake's poem "Tyger, Tyger," he explores an imagined scenario about India, where Muslim leaders begin attacking Britain in the wake of the French Revolution's vacuum of power. Although he was defeated by General Monro in 1792, everything takes on a sense of Buddhist cyclical nature when the British public learns that the general's son was killed by an Indian tiger in the same year.[2] "Tyger, Tyger" shows not only the death of the young man but also symbolically represents India.[3]

This is just a small example, yet Blake's works contain numerous images that are derived from India. From poetry to theological frameworks, from imagery to characters, these vast and lengthy details together construct Blake's understanding of the East.

---

1 Anthony Blunt, The Art of William Blake in William Blake (1757 -1827): A Catalogue of the Works of William Blake in the Tate Gallery (The Tate gallery)
2 William Blake, Tyger Tyger (Penguin Classics, 2016)
3 David Weir, Brahma in the West: William Blake and the Oriental Renaissance (State University of New York Press, 2003)

So why did Blake choose figures like Pitt and Nelson for his creations? Are they truly heroes, or are they merely ironic devices employed by Blake? Do the Eastern elements in his works provide a sufficient spiritual perspective?

Alternatively, did the intervention of the British Empire in India result in cultural appropriation and stereotypes? What did these elements from India bring to Blake?

Here, we will start by examining two works collected by Tate, "The Spiritual Form of Pitt Guiding Behemoth" and "The Spiritual Form of Nelson Guiding Leviathan," to explore how Blake incorporates aesthetic elements from the East into his works, challenging and expanding the boundaries of Western art.

We will analyse Blake's exhibition catalog and interpretations by renowned authors such as David Fallon, David Weir, David Bindman, and Northrop Frye. These primary and secondary sources provide the most comprehensive analysis of Blake and his symbolism.

The article will be divided into three parts. The first part will delve into Blake's exhibition in 1809, analysing the circumstances of the exhibition as a foundation for discussing the impact of these two paintings at the time. The second part will offer a deeper analysis of Blake's mythology and its similarities with Indian mythology. The third part will explore Blake's exploration of the boundaries of Western art through his works.

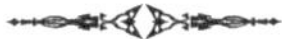

I. From Exhibitions to Artworks

In 1809, William Blake held his first and only solo exhibition on Broad Street in the Soho area of London, near Golden Square. This exhibition marked a significant turning point in his career as an artist.[4] Although the exhibition was relatively small in scale, showcasing only 16 pieces, it was a quite courageous attempt for him. Blake aimed to transform himself through this exhibition into an artist, a painter worthy of grand public projects, rather than being known solely as a writer, as he had been before. In preparation for the exhibition, Blake personally wrote a descriptive catalogue to explain his works. This catalogue served as his declaration entering the art market and as an explanation of his "poetic and historical creations," in which he aimed to revive ancient mural painting techniques.[5] In the advertisement for the exhibition, Blake mentioned the Royal Academy's bias against watercolours, which was one of the reasons he chose to privately organise this exhibition. He felt excluded from the academy system and deemed it necessary to showcase his works to the public.[6]

The reason Blake mentioned his desire to restore the ancient mural painting techniques is because his creative materials included egg tempera, which went beyond the conventional definition of watercolours. He hoped to use this method to explore more grandiose themes and, at the same time, challenge the limitations of the prevailing focus on landscape subjects in watercolour paintings during that time.[7] In his works, the depiction of figures and the elaborate watercolour style favoured by the academy were significantly different.

Blake's paintings do not belong to traditional historical genre painting; rather, his style is more like seeking the connection between his imagination and history. Just like the two works

---

4   Troy Patenaude, "'The Glory of a Nation': Recovering William Blake's 1809 Exhibition," *The British Art Journal* 4, no. 1 (2003), 52-63

5   David Erdman, The Complete Poetry and Prose of William Blake (Los Angeles and London: University of California Press, 2008), 529.

6   Erdman, 528.

7   David Blayney Brown and Martin Myrone, "William Blake's 1809 Exhibition," Tate Paper, no. 14., 1-2

highlighted in this article, "The Spiritual Form of Pitt Guiding Behemoth" and "The Spiritual Form of Nelson Guiding Leviathan," Pitt and Nelson, as modern figures, appear relatively insignificant compared to the grand ancient heroic figures.[8] However, Blake deifies them in his creations, resulting in these two works. His unique creative approach, as mentioned in the forefront of the catalogue, aims to rescue art from the hands of false colourists and ignorant connoisseurs.[9] The artistic form he advocates is precisely the modern version of the original style represented by the works showcased in the exhibition.

However, the reality is that despite the grand intentions behind Blake's works, his exhibition had a poor turnout, to the point of being dismal. There were hardly any recorded visitors of historical significance at the exhibition, except for one review published by Robert Hunt in The Examiner in September 1809.[10] This review was strongly insulting and attacking, further isolating Blake. He did not receive better reputation or gain favour from the establishment. Although he had anticipated this outcome, as indicated in the conclusion of the catalogue where he asserted his own sovereignty over his art.[11]

In 1812, a different critic from Lady's Monthly Museum provided another review of Blake's exhibited works. The value of his works was acknowledged, and the composition and colors were described as exceptionally exquisite. However, the critic found the conceptual aspect of the works to be excessively lofty, making them difficult for the audience to comprehend. This review can be seen as a mixed evaluation, offering both praise and criticism.[12] However, when considering the judgments of modern

---

8　David Erdman, The Complete Poetry and Prose of William Blake (Los Angeles and London: University of California Press, 2008), 531.

9　Erdman, 529.

10　G.E. Bentley Jr., Blake Records (Rochester: Department of English, University of Rochester, 2015), pp. 282–5.

11　David Erdman, The Complete Poetry and Prose of William Blake (Los Angeles and London: University of California Press, 2008), pp. 550.

12　G.E. Bentley Jr., Blake Records (Rochester: Department of English, University of Rochester, 2015), pp. 283

scholars regarding Blake's works, it becomes apparent that his art has transcended the confines of its time. For contemporary viewers who approach his works with modern perspectives, the meaning of the artworks becomes easier to understand and takes on a more pronounced political critique.[13] However, due to the limitations of the era, the audiences of that time found it challenging to make such assessments.

Blake's exhibitions and the artworks displayed during that time are undoubtedly regarded as great when viewed from later generations. However, his works involve numerous religious and political metaphors, making his creative intentions more enigmatic. This article aims to explore, using "The Spiritual Form of Pitt Guiding Behemoth" and "The Spiritual Form of Nelson Guiding Leviathan" as starting points, the influence of these cultural elements and information on Blake amidst the fervour of Eastern literature trends at that time. It will investigate how Blake handled this information, incorporated it into his own works, and expanded the boundaries of Western aesthetics.

In this artwork, Pitt is repeatedly portrayed in a deified manner by Blake. He is depicted as a giant figure. On the left side, stars slowly ascend into the sky. Pitt hovers magnificently above the world, with a sharp and penetrating gaze. He guides the enormous beast Behemoth. David Worrall provides a more detailed interpretation of this artwork. He believes that the figures on either side represent the "reaper" and the "plowman," symbolising the constellations of Orion and the Plough.[14] David Fallon, on the other hand, suggests that Pitt himself is depicted as a constellation, specifically the Virgo, based on the inference drawn from Pitt's robe. However, traditionally, Virgo is depicted holding two stalks of harvested wheat, a commonly seen representation symbolising the late summer season.[15] Fallon believes that Blake's

---

13 David Fallon, "That Angel Who Rides on the Whirlwind," Eighteenth-Century Life 31, no. 2 (Spring 2007): pp. 2
14 Hermione de Almeida and George H. Gilpin, Indian Renaissance, 278
15 Lily McEwan, The Art of Cartography: Cartes-à-figures (University of Missouri, 2021).

inclusion of Pitt as a constellation is a sarcastic response to Pitt's war efforts, and this image would further incite opposition and radical factions to confront him. Pitt's head is adorned with seven planets, an image that some scholars interpret as a form of self-renunciation akin to an ascetic. The crowd at Pitt's feet has been interpreted by some scholars as a representation of his suppression of civil liberties. Behind his head, a massive halo is placed, resembling a serpent intertwined, yet also resembling the sun. This effect strongly resembles the halo of Shiva in D'Hancarville, the renowned Hindu god of destruction. Blake breaks away from the classical composition of focusing the figures' gazes solely on a deified hero. Although the reaper and plowman face Pitt, only a few insignificant figures look up at him. Rather than the prayerful attitude found in traditional religious paintings, this conveys a sense of fear.[16] The surrounding destruction draws the viewer's attention away from the central figure, weakening the unity that the entire painting should possess.

In William Blake's "Descriptive Catalogue," he describes this painting as an angel capable of executing the commands of an omnipotent God, harnessing storms, and commanding wars. Such a description indeed seems like a layer of outer clothing, depicting Pitt as a person chosen by God himself and cloaked in a divine disguise. However, Fallon, at the same time, believes that this portrayal is imbued with a sense of action. Pitt harnesses hurricanes and commands storms, much like his manner of waging war. For some observers, Blake's ambiguous title suggests the apocalyptic angel of the Book of Revelation, thereby implying that the former Prime Minister is an agent of judgment, while others can reasonably interpret it as a critique of the chosen people of God. Pitt is depicted as a mediator between man and God. Blake's characterisation model is based on those who seek revenge on the envious God of September, which appears to be

---

16 Paul Barlow, The Aryan Blake: Hinduism, Art and Revelation in William Blake's Pitt and Nelson Paintings (Visual Culture in Britain, 2011), 279.

an obvious suggestion that the role Pitt is shaped into leans more toward that of a death angel.[17]

Some scholars argue that Blake's creation of "Pitt" and "Nelson" was influenced by the sculpture commemoration trend that took place between 1806 and 1807. The government and the Corporation of London launched a competition for the Nelson statue to commemorate these two heroes.[18] Blake was interested in these national projects, as mentioned earlier, and he hoped to secure government resources for grand public projects himself. In the "Descriptive Catalogue," he explicitly compared the figures in his paintings to ancient sculptures. This is a manifestation of mythologizing contemporary figures, drawing parallels with the divine figures in ancient sculpture. However, unlike the prevailing Greek and Roman sculptures, he found the works from Asia more appealing and greater.[19] He associated these exotic images with the Saviour of Christian Protestant nations.

Transcendence is the process of transforming humans into semi-divine or divine beings, and Blake considers it an important cultural reference in his creative work. It is often associated with funerals and posthumous rituals, with numerous examples in Hinduism where humans are deified. Characters like Krishna in the Hindu epic Mahabharata and Rama in the Ramayana are examples of humans becoming gods. Transcendence can be seen as a religious doctrine and also as a cultural and aesthetic commemoration. Individuals honoured with transcendence are incorporated into the temple of heroes, and the influence of them endures to this day.[20] However, 18th-century comparative theologians and historians often viewed these forms as the result of ancient religious corruption, particularly influenced by Eastern pagan worship. They believed that posthumous transcendence

---

17 William Blake, Descriptive Catalogue, (New York: Doubleday, 1988), 530.

18 Alison Yarrington, The Commemoration of the Hero, 1800–1864: Monuments to the British Victors of the Napoleonic Wars (London: Garland, 1988), viii.

19 William Blake, Descriptive Catalogue 1809, (A Woodstock Facsimile, 1990), 11

20 David Fallon, "That Angel Who Rides on the Whirlwind," *Eighteenth-Century Life* 31, no. 2 (Spring 2007), 4

originated from the ancient Chaldean worship of celestial bodies, leading to the development of Sabeanism, where people worshiped the deceased and powerful individuals. These viewpoints were not unfamiliar to Blake, who may have attended lectures at the Royal Academy where the discussion involved Sabeanism as a primitive religious error and transcendence as its subsequent idolatrous manifestation.[21] Blake's aversion to transcendence reflects his love for the democratic spirit, as the idea of elevating individuals to a status beyond humanity is repugnant to him.

The concept of sublimity is very important in "Pitt.", it is indeed evident how the concept of sublimity plays a significant role in "Pitt." However, Blake's disdain for this concept and its contrasting application in his actual practice create a stark contrast. Such a result is difficult to be understood as anything other than a rebellion, a form of veiled criticism and praise in disguise.

Transcendence itself is a significant element in Hinduism. Transcendence refers to surpassing the limitations of human existence and reaching a higher level of connection with the divine. It expresses the concept of going beyond everyday reality and human boundaries, and becomes a pursuit of the sacred and universal truths.[22] Therefore, apart from these specific artworks, Blake's ideas are almost in line with Hindu culture, as both present similar insights into transcending time and cosmic understanding, thereby introducing an exploration of spiritual truths.[23]

Different scholars have varying perspectives on the nature of Blake's works. However, it can be affirmed that his works contain a strong religious element. Northrop Frye believed that Blake's works consistently avoided direct engagement with politics and leaned more towards aesthetics and the inner self. Frye's analysis, as summarised in "Fearful Symmetry," suggests that Blake viewed

---

21 Thomas Maurice's Indian Antiques, 5 vols. (London: published by the author, 1793–1800), 2, 83–130
22 Brian K. Smith, Exorcising the Transcendent: Strategies for Defining Hinduism and Religion (The University of Chicago Press, 1987), 32-55
23 William Blake, Descriptive Catalogue, 43, in Complete Poetry and Prose, 543

natural theology as a revolutionary force that inspired the American and French revolutions. However, he also highlighted the limitations of natural theology and its repressive attitude towards imagination. Blake sympathised with the revolution but expressed skepticism regarding revolutionaries' understanding of creation and a better world. He criticised an improper attitude towards freedom, viewing it as mundane standardisation and complacent docility. Blake believed that the material world was insufficient for the imagination and emphasised the need for individuals to transcend themselves. He warned that natural religion would ultimately lead to societal corruption and degradation. Blake held a critical viewpoint on revolution and freedom, emphasising the importance of imagination and transcending the personal self.[24] From Frye's standpoint, it seems that Blake employed a strategy of shifting emphasis, moving the focus from the pros and cons of revolution to the realm of imagination and discussions on the self.

However, Frye's interpretation of "The Spiritual Form of Pitt Guiding Behemoth" and "The Spiritual Form of Nelson Guiding Leviathan" contradicts his previous views. He believes that Blake's works explore symbolic information found in the Book of Revelation. In the Book of Revelation, Behemoth and Leviathan are symbolically associated with many notorious tyrants throughout history. Blake incorporates these imagery into his own works, guided by Pitt and Nelson. These figures carry political and symbolic significance, challenging the traditional norms. The Pitt and Nelson depicted in Blake's paintings are neither divinely endowed humans as implied in Blake's commentary, nor are they orthodox demonic figures.[25]

David Erdman, on the other hand, holds an opposing stance regarding Blake, as he believes that Blake's works carry a strong political significance. For instance, in Erdman's interpretation of "The Song of Los," the people are seen encouraging the Foxtie

---

24 Northrop Frye, Fearful Symmetry - A Study of William Blake (Princeton: Princeton University Press, 1974), 66-67.
25 Northrop Frye, 'Blake's Biblical Illustrations', in The Eternal Act of Creation: Essays, 1979–1990 (Bloomington: Indiana University Press, 1993), 77.

Whigs to challenge the government's restrictions on workers' wages.[26] Erdman argues that Blake attributes political disputes such as wage exploitation and grain monopolies to the king and advisors, thereby revealing Blake's evident political stance and advocacy. Meanwhile, Erdman also cites similar views from other authors in his book. For instance, Edgar Wind suggests that Nelson represents the condemnation of dramatising his adventures to praise heroes, while Mark Schorer states that Leviathan symbolises tyrannical states.[27]

Moreover, "The Song of Los" serves as direct evidence that Blake indeed had a deep interest in and attempted to understand the experiences of the East. Whether it is Blake's Albion and Jerusalem, his England, or his Urizen and Eden, the geographical relative positions described by Blake hold symbolic significance. With his argument of the interconnection between the centre and the periphery, Blake's "map" also possesses a sufficient universality. For someone like Blake, who priorities symbolic meaning, it isinevitable to interpret any hint between Eastern locations as carrying some kind of significance. Of course, many phenomena from the so-called Eastern cultures may be intertwined to create the East that he requires. When it comes to the question of where Blake's "East" lies, a clear reference can be found in "The Song of Los," where Asia is mentioned.[28] If we judge based on the geographical references provided therein, Blake's Asia corresponds to the historical Near East, including the Ararat Mountains, encompassing the Jewish and Edenic realms. However, Asia is also depicted in the chapter of "Africa" in the book. It describes Eden, the Ararat Mountains, Chaldea, Mohammed receiving "a loose Bible," and even Brama studying philosophy in the "East."

Morton Paley links Blake's artworks to the ancient classical and Egyptian sculptures he encountered during his studies at

---

26 David Erdman, Blake: Prophet against Empire (Princeton, NJ: Princeton University Press, 1977; New York: Dover, 1991), 450.

27 Erdman, 450.

28 The Complete Poetry and Prose of William Blake, ed. by David V. Erdman (New York: Anchor Doubleday, 1988), 68–70.

the Royal Academy of Arts. He specifically mentions works such as "Parallel Lines of Artists," "Interpretation and Description of Antiquities," and "Antique Collection of Egypt, Etruria, Greece, and Rome" that discuss ancient art. Additionally, the popular depictions of Persepolis sculptures at the time also influenced Blake.[29] However, Paley fails to recognise the real significance of Blake's choice to use Eastern sculpture models, particularly those from Indian ruins. Blake's paintings attracted the interest of Academy members in Eastern art and played a role in critiquing Prime Minister Pitt's tenure and legacy.

Blake's mention of Asia in the second entry of "Descriptive Catalogue" aligns closely with the previous discussion. Such text undoubtedly broadens the scope of Asia, even encompassing India and Persia. Blake appears to be open to the concept of India, Persia, and Egypt being ancient nations but desires to designate the Near East, which includes Eden, as the supreme origin point. Furthermore, the connection between the region encompassing Israel and Judaism with "Asia" suggests that Blake is seeking Eastern associations for Hebrew art.[30] In Blake's time, this seemed to be a strategy of idealising of East, involving bold assumptions about power and imagery, and drawing comparisons between Hebrew poetry and other "Eastern" poetry.

Not only Blake, but many others also have blurred the geographical boundaries of the East. The concept of the East itself is subject to debate. Where exactly was the East defined during the 18th and 19th centuries? For American society, the East is often understood as the Far East dominated by China and Japan culturally. In contrast, for the French, British, and other European colonisers, the scope of the East is much broader. It can encompass Europe's largest, wealthiest, and oldest colonies.[31] The significance of the East for the colonisers is immense as this almost mythical concept helps them define their own culture, albeit as a distinct

29 Mary Jackson, Blake and Zoroastrianism, 1977, 72-95
30 Thomas Harmer, The Outline of A Commentary on Solomon's Song Drawn by the help of Instructions from the East (London, 1768), xii–xvi.
31 Edward W. Said, Orientalism (Penguin Classics, 2003), 32

contrast. The East, both as a cultural concept and not just a creation of the colonisers' imagination, has become an inseparable part of European material and intellectual civilisation. Eastern culture, as a discourse pattern of the West, has even been used at times to support colonial bureaucratic institutions and colonial styles.[32]

There is no denying the direct relationship between Oriental stereotypes and the British Empire's intervention in India. By the late 18th century, the works of Sir William Jones, a linguist and chief of the Bengal Asiatic Society, on Hinduism had gained widespread recognition. Weir suggests that Jones's "On the Gods of Greece, Italy, and India" profoundly influenced Blake's creation of "The Marriage of Heaven and Hell" and his study of Eastern beliefs. Furthermore, Blake's radicalism is closely connected to the republican and liberal ideas prevalent in Asian studies at the time. Jones was one of the first to propose the common origin of Sanskrit, Greek, and Latin languages and discovered the Indo-European language family. He extensively commented on and translated Indian literature and embarked on compiling Indian law. This argument can be traced to the views of Indian writers in the early 20th century who frequently made similar claims and garnered attention from influential Blake scholars interested in Indian thought, such as Yeats. It was through Jones that Blake developed a deep fascination with India. The key visual creations and references in Blake's "Jerusalem" can also be traced back to Edward Moor's "The Hindu Pantheon."[33]

The illustrations in Edward Moor's "The Hindu Pantheon" were drawn by Blake.[34] Some of the designs in the illustrations bear a striking resemblance to certain aspects of Pitt and Nelson. The flaming sources surrounding the Sun God in the illustrations share a great similarity with Pitt's halo, which is also composed of several circles. Such halos are more commonly seen in depictions

---

32 David Weir, Brahma in the West: William Blake and the Oriental Renaissance (State University of New York Press, 2003), 5

33 David Weir, Brahma in the West: William Blake and the Oriental Renaissance (State University of New York Press, 2003), 83

34 Hermione de Almeida and George H. Gilpin, Indian Renaissance (Taylor & Francis Ltd, 2016), 276

of the Buddha. In Buddha's iconography, they are often placed at the centre of smaller figures, who surround him. These figures are usually depicted worshipping the Buddha, yearning to be led by him into the realm of ultimate bliss. This aspect is similar to Pitt as portrayed by Blake, standing amidst a complex cycle of life and death, with an expressionless face, while people raise their arms in prayer to him.

Compared to Pitt's subtle intentions, Nelson's image may be more accurate and easier to find references for. Nelson's appearance closely resembles one of the most common sculptures in Hindu tradition, known as Taraka. He is called the "King of Dance" and is an incarnation of Shiva, often depicted as the destroyer god. The most accurate criterion for identifying him is the presence of dynamic and unstable features in the depiction. Shiva's typical form is depicted with one leg lifted and the other placed on a figure below. His hands are extended, each holding different symbolic patterns. Some depictions also incorporate elements of flames, representing Shiva's dance within the eternal fire and symbolising the inherent uncertainty of all things. Nelson places his conquering and destructive powers upon a restrained figure. Even the flame-like form behind the contorted serpent Leviathan shares similarities with the flames on Shiva's circular halo. It is evident how much the classic imagery of Hinduism has assisted Blake in his creations.[35]

In the 1809 exhibition, there were rumours of a third painting in the same series called Spiritual Form of Napoleon. However, many scholars believe that Blake did not create the image of Napoleon because mythologizing Napoleon had political risks associated with it. Such an act would also diminish Blake's pure patriotic intentions towards Pitt and Nelson.[36] Additionally, in 1809, Napoleon was still alive while Pitt and Nelson had already passed away. Pitt and Nelson are depicted in the artworks guiding

---

35 James Gillray, Disciples Catching the Mantle: The Spirit of Darkness
   Overshadowing the Priests of Baal (June 1808)

36 Hermione de Almeida and George H. Gilpin, Indian Renaissance (Taylor &
   Francis Ltd, 2016), 279

the biblical beasts Behemoth and Leviathan, respectively. This actually indicates that these two works existed as a series, as these two monstrous creatures are described in the Book of Job as rulers of the earth and the sea. They are symbols of God's display of power. Blake's Nelson accomplishes what God instructs Job to do, which is to bind the nose of Leviathan with a cord. Nelson effortlessly holds the rope, thereby enveloping the innocent people of the world in the beast. In Blake's Jerusalem, created in 1804, he also mentions these two monstrous creatures and uses vocabulary that aligns with his depiction of Nelson and Pitt: "Leviathan/And Behemoth, the War by sea enormous, and the war/By land astounding."[37] Although this statement does not directly define whether Blake likens these figures to heroes, the beasts play a significant role in the text of Revelation, symbolising the forces that foreshadow the end of the world,[38] thus demonstrating their close connection to Blake's concept of the New Jerusalem.

Furthermore, in the descriptions of the painting related to Napoleon, there is no mention of the central figure exerting control over beings in any way. This is also the main distinction between the depiction of Napoleon and Pitt and Nelson. This viewpoint is acknowledged by David Bindman, who believes that while the original intentions behind the creation of Nelson and Pitt may be debatable, it is undeniable that their visual effects align with the majestic and divine images in the Bible, representing the individuals leading humanity towards the final judgment.[39] His perspective aligns with that of Anthony Blunt, who argues that Pitt and Nelson were incorporated by Blake into his own mythological system as symbols of transcendence, representing Los - the Spirit and Tharmas - the Sense.[40] Blake's works during this period seem to have transcended the societal framework of the time, as he sought to address social issues according to the plan set by God.

---

37 William Blake, Jerusalem: The Emanation of the Great Albion (London, 1804), chapter 4, lines 38-40
38 The Book of Enoch, ed. Matthew Black (Leiden: Brill, 1985), 97
39 Bindman, David, Blake as an Artist (Phaeton Press LTD., 1977), 163
40 Anthony Blunt, The Art of William Blake (London: Oxford University Press, 1959), 97

The available records indicate that Napoleon was depicted as a powerful figure, with his hands grasping the sun and moon, while one foot was chained to the ground, and the foreground depicted a road paved with corpses.[41] Here, we see a departure from the portrayal of Pitt and Nelson. In the paintings of Pitt and Nelson, although the victims are suffering, they are still alive. Additionally, the imagery of figures being bound to the ground is a recurring feature in Blake's works, with the most famous example being "The Good and Evil Angels" painted in 1795. This artwork depicts a benevolent angel protecting a child from the harm of an evil angel, with the latter being bound by chains. Similarly, in Blake's poem "Visions of the Daughters of Albion" created in 1793, Oothoon and her assailant Bromion are also depicted bound together. The use of chains as one of Blake's longstanding intentions expresses the idea that all energies can be corrupted into forms of power. This aligns well with the theme of Napoleon. Most scholars interpret the binding with iron chains as a symbol of the transformation of imperial power brought about by the European wars and revolutions.[42] However, considering the context of the expansion of the British Empire at that time, the imagery from Hinduism can also be interpreted differently.

Blake often used the term "empire," mostly implying the potential corruption of existing empires but also expressing his imagination of a glorious empire.[43] This concept aligns with the Christian notion of the coming of Christ establishing the "City of God" or the New Jerusalem. An ideal spiritual empire is always in a state of perfection. He has other artworks that testify to this possibility of overlap with Christianity. While creating Pitt and Nelson, he also produced several versions of "A Vision of the Last Judgement."[44] His intention was to depict judgment, describing the

---

41 H.H. Statham, The Blake Drawings at the Burlington Fine Art Club (1876)
42 Anne Kostelanetz Mellor, Blake's Human Form Divine (Berkeley and London: University of California Press, 1974), 149
43 Saree Makdisi, William Blake and he Impossible History of the 1790s (University of Chicago Press 2002)
44 Alan Jacobs, Everything is Illuminated, 2020

judgment of individuals through the recognition of their spiritual state.

Napoleon was sometimes defined as an anti-Christian figure[45], so his downfall was seen as paving the way for the arrival of a brighter future. In such a historical context, it can explain the contradictions in Pitt and Nelson. They appear to celebrate the containment of Napoleon by Pitt and Nelson while also portraying the victors as representatives of destroy.[46] As mentioned earlier in "The Song of Los," Los obtaining the Quran in the text implies a transcendent power that unifies the world.[47] In the contemporary context, Blake's incorporation of Indian imagery can be understood as a clear analogy to the absorption of Indian spirituality and cultural traditions by the British Empire, but it also represents a destructive act. His depiction of Pitt and Nelson can be interpreted through the imagery of Krishna, Shiva, and the Buddha, who are described as dancing or meditating amid the death of the world. In the Mahabharata, Krishna ultimately reveals his true spiritual state as the center of the cycle of life and death, where unpredictable destruction is an inevitable part of the process. Blake himself seems to have integrated elements of Hindu concepts of reincarnation and dharma in "A Vision of the Last Judgement." The idea presented by Wilkins, who sought to challenge Hinduism by introducing the concept of the "collapse of polytheism,"[48] suggests that individuals traverse states through eternal motion or the process of rebirth.

Wilkins' approach involved attempting to construct a framework for interpreting world mythology, but the premise of this framework was to treat the content of the Bible as factual and merge it with other classical texts. As a result, any interpretation of mythologies that did not align with Christianity would distort events. This analytical system ensured the supreme status of

---

45 Stuart Semmel, Napoleon and the British (New Haven, CT, and London: Yale University Press, 2004)

46 David Erdman, Blake: Prophet against Empire (Princeton, NJ: Princeton University Press, 1977; New York: Dover, 1991), 453–4

47 Blake, William, Selected Poetry, (Penguin Classics, *2019)*

48 Bhagvat-Geeta, 23–5

Judeo-Christian beliefs while also connecting the evolution of civilisation and human migrations, ultimately compiling a global history book.[49] Through the dissemination of imperial and universal knowledge, the history of Christianity became part of globalisation.

Blake also incorporated Nelson and Pitt into the framework of the Bible by having them guide monsters, thus connecting them with the spiritual concepts of India. The wars initiated by these figures also secured these concepts for Britain. However, what Blake demonstrates as the sublimity of the Bible is actually a transformation of the sublime derived from Hinduism. His art is activated through the imagery of Hinduism, continuing to provide fuel for his imagination. Within Blake's mythological framework, the Bible and the Hindu scriptures blend together, forming a unique understanding. He believes that these texts are revelations, explaining spiritual truths on different levels. His art attempts to break traditional religious boundaries, integrating diverse cultural and religious elements to convey a shared human ideal.

These Spiritual Forms represent Blake's integration of Indian and Christian beliefs in the new era through the individuals who embody these ideals. He, like a true Christian, believes Pitt to be the angel of revelation, and also, like a true Hindu, believes Pitt and Nelson to be agents of Dharma. The impact of his actions is profound. The cultural connections between Hinduism and Europe were later proposed by Max Muller after Blake's death. The pagan beliefs of Europe, the Zoroastrianism of Iran, the Vedic religion that preceded Hinduism and Buddhism—all of these are part of a common Aryan mythology. The source of Indian mythology does not lie in the Bible but in the "original Aryans" who evolved from their homeland into the cultures of India, Persia, Greece, Rome, the Celts, and the Germanic peoples.[50]

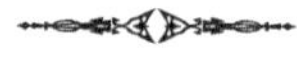

---

49 Paul Barlow, The Aryan Blake: Hinduism, Art and Revelation in William Blake's Pitt and Nelson Paintings (Visual Culture in Britain, 2011), 289.
50 Max Muller, Lectures on the Origin and Growth of Religion (London: Longmans, Green, 1898–1907), 259.

II. Myths and Mythologies: Links in Similarity

The previous passage briefly described the paintings by Pitt and Nelson, as well as the relationship between them and elements of Eastern culture. In the 18th to 19th centuries, the British Empire was a vast colonial empire that controlled regions like India in the East. Viewing Eastern countries and cultures as conquered and occupied entities, romanticising, exorcizing, and idealising them, was part of the mainstream culture at the time. However, this also made them victims of imperialist rule.

Blake's incorporation of Indian imagery can be understood as a form of resistance and criticism against imperialism. By using Indian imagery and symbols, he revealed the destruction and devastation brought about by the British Empire's colonial rule in India. This absorption implies that imperialism attempted to assimilate India's spiritual and cultural traditions into its own, but in reality, it was an exploitation of Indian culture. In Blake's perspective, this was a destructive act and a vivid expression of his strong criticism and opposition to imperialism.

However, influenced by the era and geography, Blake had a limited perspective on Indian culture. Additionally, Blake regarded India as a wellspring for his own creative inspiration, a boundless source of ideas for him. Of course, this is not his fault, as in the last ten years of the 18th century, in response to the monumental works of William Jones and other members of the Asiatic Society, there was a significant surge of researchers engaging in mythological studies of Hindu deities. Furthermore, publishers capitalised on scholars' heightened interest in Indian literature by releasing new editions of previously published materials. Blake must have been one of the readers, as his poetry demonstrates that he shared similar perspectives and ideas with these mythologists studying Indian myths, along with some distinctly "Indian" imagery and metaphors.[51] During that time, William Jones was the most authoritative scholar, and thus Blake's works would bear resemblances to Jones' viewpoints.

---

51 David Weir, Brama in the West (State University of New York Press 2003), 55

Although Jones's mythological research was conducted in India, his investigations and theories were well-known in London.[52] Blake's portrayal of Wilkins translating Indian classics was inspired by scenes depicting Jones translating Indian law. In Jones's "On the Gods of Greece, Italy, and India," details about Indian mythology that had never been disclosed before were provided.[53] These details bear similarities to Blake's mythological system. This is undoubtedly direct evidence that Jones's texts did influence the formation of Blake's mythological perspective. For example, in Blake's epic works, destruction and chaos are caused by the giant Albion. Albion's slumber allows Luvah to steal the Horse of Light from Urizen, triggering a great flood that engulfs the slumbering giant.[54] Similarly, in Jones's translation and interpretation of the Bhagavat Purana, there are descriptions of similar mythological events. The slumber of Vishnu triggers a cataclysm that nearly destroys the world. All of Vishnu's creations are engulfed in an ocean. While the theft depicted in Blake's narrative may have originated from the Prometheus myth in Greek mythology, the inclusion of slumber and flood in Blake's mythology aligns closely with Jones's Indian mythology.[55]

Another similarity between Blake's mythology and Hinduism is the presence of guardian figures who protect the creations from complete destruction. In Blake's works, the protector is Los, who temporarily embodies as the protective primordial being of divine humanity.[56] In the Bhagavat Purana, the protector is Hari.[57] However, Jones further revealed the more prominent name in Hindu mythology, Vishnu. Vishnu, along with the creator Brahma and the destroyer Shiva, forms the trinity of major deities in Hinduism. The three of them represent the forces of creation,

---

52 John Drew, India and the Romantic Imagination (Delhi and New York: Oxford University Press, 1987) 143

53 William Jones, On the Gods of Greece, Italy, and India (Cambridge University Press, 2014)

54 William Blake, Jerusalem: The Emanation of The Giant Albion, (Kessinger Publishing Co. 2004)

55 David Weir, Brama in the West (State University of New York Press 2003), 58

56 William Blake, The Song of Los in Selected Poetry, (Penguin Classics, *2019)*

57 William Jones, Bhagavat Purana

preservation, and destruction. Although Jones's interpretation of Hindu mythology differs from Blake's original mythology because Jones acknowledges the superiority of the Christian tradition. In contrast, Blake's own mythology serves as a critique of the institutionalised religion present in his time. His purpose is to present alternative systems to replace this religion.[58] Blake's opposition to the form of national religion also drove him to explore Eastern mythology as a starting point for his critique.

One point that both Maurice and Blake touch upon is the Indian myth of the "Mundane Egg." Blake has undergone multiple evolutions of the Mundane Egg in his poetry, starting from "The Four Zoas" and approaching a version closer to Hinduism in "Jerusalem." The world is created from the egg. This concept was quite prevalent in theological studies of the late 18th century.[59]

Blake's inclination towards religion places him in a highly advantageous position, enabling him to appreciate the liberating empathy towards the Hindu system that emerged in the late 18th century. By comparing the theological theories of Brahmanism and Christianity, the British intensified the debate on the origins of religion and the authenticity of scriptures. Blake repeatedly drew inspiration from Wilkins' translations of scriptures, indicating that he considered this classic work as a new Bible. Thus, in his conception, Hindu ceremonies could be seen alongside the Hebrew Bible and the Christian New Testament as another collection manipulated by priests to establish laws and regulations. This attitude may not necessarily reflect Wilkins' stance, but he did acknowledge the potential corruption of the pure beliefs of Hinduism by the priestly class. William Jones' research also greatly assisted Blake in creating his own religious system. Similar to Wilkins, Jones also divided religion into two levels: the spiritual and the ritualistic practices. This division

---

58 Maja Pašović, "Hold Infinity in the palm of your hand And Eternity in an hour": William Blake's Visions of Time and Space in the Light of Eastern Traditions (University of Waterloo, 2013), 133

59 A. D. Nuttall, The Alternative Trinity: Gnostic Heresy in Marlowe, Milton, and Blake (Oxford: Clarendon Press, 1998), 11. In Kathleen Raine, Blake and Tradition, 2 vols. (Princeton: Princeton University Press, 1968)

allowed readers to focus on the philosophical core of Hinduism. For Jones, the multitude of Hindu deities and the diverse nature of the universe were essentially created from the same substance, or more precisely, from the same energy, as divine energy could only manifest in material form to a significant extent for ordinary individuals. This line of thought aligns well with Blake's theological framework. However, Blake did not necessarily need to incorporate these ideas into his creative mythologies, just as he did not require Wilkins to bring counter-legalistic significance to myths. Yet, the counter-legalistic narratives woven into the Hindu theological accounts circulating during Blake's time undoubtedly piqued the interest of someone like Blake. This is because such a reversal greatly bolstered the grandeur of Blake's theology.

Of course, there were also individuals like Maurice who believed that Hinduism posed a threat to national stability. Undoubtedly concerned about the political implications, Maurice vigorously criticised Brahmanic beliefs. However, his actions inadvertently provided a platform for the promotion of Indology. This also offered Blake a new context in which to express his creations. Thus, in Blake's era, the theological aspects of Hindu mythology helped him unravel his own overarching narrative and even provided excellent source material for future generations. The spiritual essence from India, to some extent, assisted Blake in his endeavours. Blake's borrowing and reinterpretation undoubtedly made him one of the greatest beneficiaries.

From this, it can be seen that Los exists as a crucial link between the Blakean mythos and Indian mythology. The above discussion indeed demonstrates the influence of Indian mythology on Blake's creation. Blake drew sufficient knowledge and energy from it, which became stepping stones on his path to becoming an artist. Hinduism helped Blake organise his mythological structure and lay down the fundamental framework, upon which his theories could expand limitlessly. The awe-inspiring details in his works transformed into his most refined explanations.

III. Los and Brahma: Reshaping the Boundaries of Western Art

In the previous chapter, we discussed how Blake's mythological system likely drew inspiration from certain aspects of Hindu mythology. However, due to the limitations of population and information flow at that time, it is difficult to ascertain whether Blake himself had a correct understanding of the doctrines or concepts within Hinduism. In this chapter, we will use different examples to determine whether Blake's judgment of Hindu ideas includes stereotypes.

First, let's analyse the concept of time. In the classic Indian text, Maitri Upanishad, time is defined as two aspects of Brahman: temporal and timeless. The timeless aspect is eternal, serving as the vessel for the divine, possessing unparalleled divine power and immutability. All things originate from Brahman or time. In the Upanishad, time refers to the moment that has existed since the birth of the world and continues to exist forever. Brahman's time and timeless aspect are applied in the creation and rotation of the solar system. Prior to the emergence of the sun, there is Akala, the timeless aspect. Once the sun emerges, Sakala, time, appears.[60] This concept may seem confusing, but a simpler explanation is that the timeless aspect represents a form of Brahman, existing as the conveyer of truth and having the potential for eternal existence in the world.[61] The timeless Brahman consists of timeless units of time, where the duration of moments is not determined by temporal duration but by assimilating into eternity through self-knowledge. In the Bhagavad Gita, Krishna states that attaining self-knowledge and realising the path to the ultimate truth is the highest and supreme art.[62]

Certainly, it can be said that Blake made efforts to steer people away from a secular conception of time towards a divine conception of time, leading him to struggle against ideas based on a continuous historical process.[63] Therefore, he attempted

---

60 Seyyed Hossein Nasr, Knowledge and the Sacred (State University of New York Press), 198

61 Anada Coomaraswamy, Time and Eternity (Munshiram Manoharlal Publishers 1993), 15

62 David Wilkins, The Bhagvat-Geeta, 78

63 William Blake, The complete Poetry and Prose of William Blake, 127

to restore past beauty and sublimity and ultimately guide our perception beyond the eternal death of the secular world. Drawing upon Indian concepts that classify the universe into four ages, Blake created four cycles of human history within the realms of Eden, Beulah, Generation, and Ulro. These worlds are often seen as different states of the human spirit or interchangeable spaces where humans reside or descend, and they can also be seen as different "levels of imagination." Blake's idea was to recreate the four cycles needed in human history, which is vividly expressed in his depiction of Eden and the world of Ulro, which are extreme opposites. Percy Bysshe Shelley points out that "one extreme is the determinate and complete reality of Eden, the world of eternal life; the other is the visionary chaos of Ulro, the world of eternal death." In the Indian cosmology, the Krita Yuga (also known as Satya Yuga) is the world of eternal life, encompassing all beauty and sublimity that revolves around it, while the Kali Yuga is the world of eternal suffering and death. Blake mentions on multiple occasions his characters entering the realm of Ulro, such as Milton and Oothoon, where the illusion of materialism and false appearances are seen as reality. The time in Ulro is in a perpetual state of progress, but it does not progress towards beauty, spiritual cognition, and the realm of eternity.[64] Ulro's world is trapped in its own time, a product of scientific laws and the denial of divine intervention. Ulro is called the "world of death," not merely because everything dies there, but because they have 'died' to eternity. This is why Ulro is also the world of iron. In Blake's design of "The Four Zoas" depicted in "Milton," he reveals that Urizen usually occupies the southern region, representing the world of Ulro. Although the primary metal associated with Urizen is "gold,"[65] symbolizing the primary materialistic characteristics of the earthly world, Blake often associates iron—the metal of destruction—with Urizen.

Compared to the limitations of all the spatial and temporal constraints of human life reflected in Urizen's "book of iron,"

---

64 Foster, Damon, A Blake Dictionary: The Ideas and Symbols of William Blake (Brown, 1988), 416
65 Damon, 419

Los embodies imagination and spiritual revolution, guiding the existence of joy and peace experienced by humanity on Earth. Nasr states in his work "Knowledge and the Sacred," this joy and tranquility are nothing but signs of the eternal touching the human soul.[66] While Urizen uses his "book of iron" to impose his laws and doctrines upon the inhabitants of the Earth, suppressing the use of imagination, Los, on the other hand, exalts the eternal through his songs and strength, creating the armour of science and advocating fighting for wisdom.[67] Los and Orc's position is in the north, where the world of Eden resides. Interestingly, although both Los and Orc are associated with the metal iron and depicted as blacksmiths, the world of Eden they sometimes inhabit is bathed in "golden mountains" and "pinnacles of palaces." In contrast to the darkness and despair, symbolised as the "cruelty of Urizen" and the "loom of Locke, washed by the waterwheel of Newton," the existence in Eden is synonymous with eternal life. Furthermore, Eden is a dwelling place of spirituality and understanding of divine powers: it is the highest state, the union of the Creator with the created, energy with form. In Blake's symbolism, the Eden of his symbolic system is a "city of fiery spiritual sun." In contrast to the limited time in Urizen, time in Eden is free from past and future disturbances; instead, it expands perpetually as infinite moments. In the world of Eden, there is a near-divine vision, and the brotherhood of humanity integrates every small detail of life into a unified whole.[68] Same as the Golden Age or Krta Yuga, when time is seen as leading humanity back to the unity with divine existence or eternity, time in the world of Eden serves the purpose of purifying the soul and bringing it back to the origin of the universe.

Blake's assertion, "A gate to Eden emerges every two hundred years,"[69] exposes his comprehension of Eden. According to Blake, Eden represents a realm of perpetual existence where

---

66 Nasr, Knowledge and the Sacred, 195
67 William Blake, The Complete Poetry and Prose of William Blake, 407
68 Blake, 174, 188, 159
69 William Blake, The Complete Poetry and Prose of William Blake, 197

time perpetually cycles back, unrestricted by actual creation. It is intriguing to note that Blake equates a two-hundred-year interval with seven ages, each encircled by "silver and golden bridges." Moreover, these ages can manifest themselves within various units of time, including minutes, hours, days, months, and years. However, within this sequence, there is a pivotal moment that holds the utmost significance due to the cyclical nature of time. This statement explains that Blake might have encountered similar concepts in Sir William Jones's "Hindu Chronology."[70] In this work, Jones explores the idea that smaller time units, as perceived through empirical thinking, can encompass longer ones. Jones goes on to explain the Hindu belief that "a year represents the day and night of the gods; it is divided into two halves, with the day when the sun moves northward and the night when the sun moves southward".[71] Symbolically, from Blake's viewpoint, Los vanishes when night befalls as he endeavors to restore the eternal and dismantle the boundless world of Urizen[72], leading to a conflict with Urizen and his formidable army. Following this confrontation, Los finds himself shackled by Urizen's oppressive laws, no longer basking in the radiance of the sun and flames (which symbolise Los's elements). Instead, he awakens to confront the curse of darkness and a world lacking eternity. Consequently, Los descends into the southern region, Urizen's realm of darkness, awaiting an ascent to the north and entrance into the imagined dominion of Eden. In "The Fourth Night of the Four Zoas," the struggle between finite, linear time and eternal time reaches its pinnacle as Los, under Urizen's control, binds time into the past, present, and future, continually merging them together. As a result, Los fails to put the seeds of cyclical time in the human psyche, but rather weaves a finite timeline in history where divine possibilities sink into the mortal realm.

In a similar manner to Urizen's decree, "Spread mighty power / From North to South,"[73] time itself retreats from its boundless

---

70 Kathleen Raine, Blake and Tradition (Princeton University Press, 1968), 144
71 William Jones, Hindu Chronology, 282
72 William Blake, The Complete Poetry and Prose of William Blake, pp. 73
73 William Blake, The Complete Poetry and Prose of William Blake, 335

and cyclic trajectory, transforming into a linear descent that eventually reaches its end. Concurrently, humanity experiences a sweeping decline in its spiritual state, engulfing the entire earthly realm. Consequently, the once inhabited Eden transforms into a desolate dwelling, while Urizen's world becomes the abode of human existence. Thus, the descent of humanity from Eden to Urizen symbolises not only the decline of imagination but also the regression of the human spirit over time, as it transitions into subsequent eras or epochs. Through his exploration of ancient Indian literature, William Jones also observed that the progress of humanity across four ages had an opposing effect, as substantial advancements in spiritual enlightenment and social progress were not achieved. Instead, humanity became increasingly mired in suffering and deterioration.This aspect deeply inspired Blake and was incorporated into the creation of most of his works. Spirituality and imagination, transcending the material world, became the crucial keys to human evolution in Blake's brushstrokes.

Therefore, Los, as an essential link between Blake's mythology and Hindu mythology, exists. The above discussion indeed demonstrates the influence of Hindu mythology on Blake's creative process. Blake drew sufficient knowledge and energy from it, which became stepping stones on his path to becoming an artist. Hinduism helped Blake structure his mythological framework and provided him with a fundamental backdrop, allowing his theories to expand infinitely within this framework. The breathtaking details in his works became the most delicate explanations for him. By incorporating elements of Hinduism, Blake expanded the boundaries of Western art. His works surpassed the traditional realm of Western art, integrating the essence of Eastern philosophy and mysticism. Through the mutual influence between Blake and Hinduism, he presented the audience with a unique artistic experience, stimulating their thoughts and imagination.

Conclusion

Certainly, "The Spiritual Form of Pitt Guiding Behemoth" and "The Spiritual Form of Nelson Guiding Leviathan" hold a special place in art history. Both works demonstrate William Blake's interest in Eastern aesthetics. The celebrity status of Pitt and Nelson was utilised to enhance the imagery, elevating them to the status of true public artworks. At the same time, these two pieces serve as powerful evidence, attesting to the spiritual vision offered by the East. The British Empire's intervention in India facilitated Blake's exposure and in-depth study of Eastern culture. He regarded India as a sacred source, both in terms of inspiration and wealth.

It is certain that "The Spiritual Form of Pitt Guiding Behemoth" and "The Spiritual Form of Nelson Guiding Leviathan" hold a special position in art history. These works embody William Blake's exploration of the sublime, a major theme in religion, throughout his creations. Influenced by the surge of sculptural monuments from 1806 to 1807, Blake mythologized figures from society and associated Asian imagery with Christianity. His aversion to the sublime reflects his love for the spirit of democracy, while his works also reveal his political stance and criticism of the government.

Blake extensively studied Eastern cultures and incorporated their symbolic significance into his works. His paintings attracted members of the academic tradition, arousing their interest in Eastern art and playing a role in the critique of Prime Minister Pitt's term and legacy. Blake's study of the East was connected to his interest in ancient cultures of India, Persia, and Egypt. Although the concept of the East is geographically vague, for Blake, it encompassed regions associated with the Garden of Eden and Hebrew culture.

Blake's works demonstrate his pursuit of borrowing from and symbolically referencing Eastern cultures while reflecting his radical stance. His interest in Indian thought may have been influenced by early Asian scholars like Sir William Jones. The designs in Blake's illustrations resemble the imagery in his paintings, incorporating references to Buddha and other Eastern figures.

In Blake's work, "The Spiritual Form of Pitt Guiding Behemoth," Pitt is depicted as a mythological giant suspended in the sky, guiding the behemoth. Other figures in the artwork symbolise reapers and tillers, while planets surround Pitt's head, representing his spiritual ascension. Observers perceive the suppression of civil liberties in the image and symbols of the god of destruction. Blake breaks away from traditional compositions, weakening the centrality of the main figure through disruption and fear.

In "The Spiritual Form of Nelson Guiding Leviathan," Nelson's figure resembles the Taraga sculptures in Hinduism, portraying the image of the king of dance corresponding to the incarnation of the destructive god Shiva. His posture and the symbolic objects in his hand align with Hindu imagery, expressing instability and the destructive power of strength. In contrast, Blake is believed to have not created an image of Napoleon due to its political risks, as it would contradict the pure patriotic intentions of the Pitt and Nelson works.

Blake's works transcend the existing social system of the time, presenting his idea of addressing social issues through God's plan. The image of Napoleon, unlike the works on Pitt and Nelson, lacks the imagery of controlling other creatures and is instead bound by iron chains. The common motif of bondage in Blake's works symbolises the corruption of energy by power, with the iron chains interpreted as the imperial transformation brought by European wars and revolutions. Blake employs the concept of empire to express the corruption of existing empires and showcases his imagination of a better empire. His works align with the concept of the new Jerusalem in Christianity, depicting the state of an ideal spiritual empire in its perfection. Elements associated with Christianity can also be observed in his works, such as "A Vision of the Last Judgement," which portrays the judgment of individuals through spiritual states of recognition.

The image of Napoleon is considered anti-Christ, and his downfall paves the way for a bright future. Blake portrays Pitt and Nelson as figures guiding monsters, intertwining them within the biblical framework and connecting them to spiritual concepts in India. Blake attempts to break religious boundaries, merging elements from different cultures and religions to convey a shared human ideal. His works have had a profound influence, fostering an understanding of cultural connections between India and Europe.

In "The Spiritual Form of Pitt Guiding Behemoth," Blake employs a technique of deification to portray Pitt, showcasing his immense figure and the power to guide the beast. The artwork presents associations with elements of Eastern culture, contrasting with the idealisation and conquest of the East under the imperial rule of the British Empire at the time. Blake incorporates Indian imagery as a means of critiquing imperialism and revealing the destructive nature of colonial domination. His work demonstrates a borrowing from Hindu mythology, influenced by early Asian scholars like Sir William Jones. Blake's mythological system, influenced by Hinduism, gives his works a unique and political significance. The parallels between Hindu mythology and the religious system created by Blake express his criticism of institutionalised religion. Blake's interest in the origins of religion and the authenticity of classics led him to merge Hinduism with the Hebrew Bible and Christianity. His interpretations of the Mundane Egg myth and his study of Hinduism strengthened his mythological system. Blake's creations were influenced by Indologists, while his works contributed to the dissemination of Hindu mythology. This mutual influence provided Blake with a new environment and background for his creations. The spiritual aspects of Hinduism hold significant importance in Blake's works, establishing him as a prominent figure in Indology studies.

Blake may have been influenced by Hinduism in his mythology, particularly in terms of concepts related to time and creation. Hinduism divides time into different ages and cycles, which Blake also reflects in his works. He emphasises the importance of creating great works in an instant and seeks to restore past golden ages. By incorporating elements of Hinduism, Blake expands the boundaries of Western art and creates a unique artistic experience. Through the mutual influence with Hinduism, Blake stimulates the audience's thoughts and imagination.

Blake not only created mythology but also turned himself into a myth. His works serve as the most direct expression of bringing Eastern culture into Western culture. The intricate details in his paintings and the beauty of his long poems serve as the keys that connect two distinct realms. And, like his name, his works will remain immortal throughout the river of time.

Bibliography

1. Barlow, Paul, The Aryan Blake: Hinduism, Art and Revelation in William Blake's Pitt and Nelson Paintings (Visual Culture in Britain, 2011)

2. Bhagvat-Geeta

3. Blake, William, Descriptive Catalogue 1809, (A Woodstock Facsimile, 1990)

4. Blake, William, Jerusalem: The Emanation of the Great Albion (London, 1804), chapter 4, lines 38-40

5. Blake, William, Selected Poetry, (Penguin Classics, *2019)*

6. Blake, William, The complete Poetry and Prose of William Blake

7. Blake, William, Tyger Tyger (Penguin Classics, 2016)

8. Blunt, Anthony, The Art of William Blake in William Blake (1757 -1827): A Catalogue of the Works of William Blake in the Tate Gallery (The Tate gallery)

9. Bentley Jr., G.E., Blake Records (Rochester: Department of English, University of Rochester, 2015)

10. Bindman, David, Blake as an Artist (Phaeton Press LTD., 1977)

11. Blunt, Anthony The Art of William Blake (London: Oxford University Press, 1959)

12. Brown, David Blayney and Myrone, Martin, "William Blake's 1809 Exhibition," Tate Papers no. 14.

13. Coomaraswamy, Anada, Time and Eternity (Munshiram Manoharlal Publishers 1993)

14. Damon, Foster, A Blake Dictionary: The Ideas and Symbols of William Blake

15. De Almeida, Hermione and Gilpin, George H., Indian Renaissance (Taylor & Francis Ltd, 2016)

16. Drew, John, India and the Romantic Imagination (Delhi and New York: Oxford University Press, 1987)

17. Erdman, David V., The Complete Poetry and Prose of William Blake (Los Angeles and London: University of California Press, 2008)

18. Fallon, David "That Angel Who Rides on the Whirlwind," Eighteenth-Century Life 31, no. 2 (Spring 2007)

19. Frye, Northrop, Fearful Symmetry - A Study of William Blake (Princeton: Princeton University Press, 1974)

20. Gillray, James, Disciples Catching the Mantle: The Spirit of Darkness Overshadowing the Priests of Baal (June 1808)

21. Harmer, Thomas, The Outline of A Commentary on Solomon's Song Drawn by the help of Instructions from the East (London, 1768)

22. Jackson, Mary, Blake and Zoroastrianism, 1977

23. Jacobs, Alan, Everything is Illuminated, 2020

24. Jones, William, On the Gods of Greece, Italy, and India (Cambridge University Press, 2014)

25. Jones, William, Hindu Chronology

26. Makdisi, Saree, William Blake and he Impossible History of the 1790s (University of Chicago Press 2002)

27. Maurice, Thomas, Indian Antiquities, 5 vols. (London: published by the author, 1793–1800), 2

28. McEwan, Lily, The Art of Cartography: Cartes-à-figures (University of Missouri, 2021)

29. Mellor, Anne Kostelanetz, Blake's Human Form Divine (Berkeley and London: University of California Press, 1974)

30. Muller, Max, Lectures on the Origin and Growth of Religion (London: Longmans, Green, 1898–1907)

31. Nasr, Seyyed Hossein, Knowledge and the Sacred (State University of New York Press, 1989)

32. Nuttall, A.D., The Alternative Trinity: Gnostic Heresy in Marlowe, Milton, and Blake (Oxford: Clarendon Press, 1998), In Kathleen Raine, Blake and Tradition, 2 vols. (Princeton: Princeton University Press, 1968

33. Pašović, Maja, Hold Infinity in the palm of your hand And Eternity in an hour: William Blake's Visions of Time and Space in the Light of Eastern Traditions (University of Waterloo, 2013)

34. Patenaude, Troy, "'The Glory of a Nation': Recovering William Blake's 1809 Exhibition," The British Art Journal 4, no. 1 (2003)

35. Raine, Kathleen, Blake and Tradition (Princeton University Press, 1968), Vol. II

36. Said, Edward W., Orientalism (Penguin Classics, 2003)

37. Semmel, Stuart, Napoleon and the British (New Haven, CT, and London: Yale University Press, 2004)

38. Smith, Brian K., Exorcising the Transcendent: Strategies for Defining Hinduism and Religion (The University of Chicago Press, 1987)

39. Statham, H.H., The Blake Drawings at the Burlington Fine Art Club (1876)

40. The Complete Poetry and Prose of William Blake, ed. by David V. Erdman (New York: Anchor Doubleday, 1988)

41. The Book of Enoch, ed. Matthew Black (Leiden: Brill, 1985)

42. Weir, David, Brahma in the West: William Blake and the Oriental Renaissance (State University of New York Press, 2003)

43. Wilkins, David, The Bhagvat-Geeta

44. Yarrington, Alison, The Commemoration of the Hero, 1800–1864: Monuments to the British Victors of the Napoleonic Wars (London: Garland, 1988), viii.

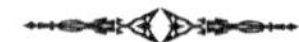